Influential Women

Malala Yousafzai

Other titles in the *Influential Women* series include:

Anne Frank
Cleopatra
Hillary Clinton
Marie Curie

Influential Women

Malala Yousafzai

Stuart A. Kallen

ReferencePoint
Press®

San Diego, CA

© 2016 ReferencePoint Press, Inc.
Printed in the United States

For more information, contact:
ReferencePoint Press, Inc.
PO Box 27779
San Diego, CA 92198
www.ReferencePointPress.com

LIBRARY OF CONGRESS CATALOGING-IN-PUBLICATION DATA

Kallen, Stuart A., 1955-
  Malala Yousafzai / by Stuart A. Kallen.
    pages cm. -- (Influential women)
  Includes bibliographical references and index.
  ISBN 978-1-60152-952-7 (hardback) -- ISBN 1-60152-952-X (hardback) 1. Yousafzai, Malala, 1997- 2. Girls--Education--Pakistan. 3. Sex discrimination in education--Pakistan. 4. Women social reformers--Pakistan--Biography. 5. Social reformers--Pakistan--Biography. 6. Political activists--Pakistan--Biography. 7. Girls--Violence against--Pakistan. I. Title.
  LC2330.K35 2016
  371.822095491--dc23
                                                          2015026635

Contents

Introduction

She Is Malala

A hero may be defined as someone who voluntarily leaves a point of safety and risks death to save others. By that definition Malala Yousafzai is undoubtedly a hero. In early 2009 Malala came to the world's attention at age eleven when she risked her life to blog for the British Broadcasting Corporation (BBC). Malala wrote about her struggle to obtain an education while living under Taliban rule in the Swat Valley in northwestern Pakistan.

The Taliban is an Islamic fundamentalist political group. Members follow a strict interpretation of sharia, or Islamic law, which imposes severe restrictions on people's behavior. The Taliban is particularly harsh in its treatment of girls and women. The group bans all female education, and those who violate the decree face flogging, torture, and execution. The restrictions resulted in the 2009 closure of Malala's school, founded by her father, education activist Ziauddin Yousafzai.

In the Spotlight

In her blogs Malala described the sound of artillery fire in the night and the fear of death threats from strangers. After her words were published on the BBC's Pakistani website, Malala found herself in the media spotlight. In 2010 she was invited to appear on a popular Pakistani television news show seen by 25 million viewers. She spoke eloquently about Pakistani girls threatened for simply wanting to attend school. In 2011 Malala became a national hero when she won Pakistan's National Youth Peace Prize. After receiving the prize, she told a radio interviewer: "All I want is an education. And I am afraid of no one."[1]

Going public brought great danger. Malala's family received numerous death threats, and Malala in particular was targeted for execution by the Taliban. In October 2012 fifteen-year-old Malala was shot in the head by a masked gunman while she was riding the bus home from school. The bullet cut a path along the exterior of Malala's skull and went through her neck but miraculously did not kill her. She was treated in a Pakistani hospital and then moved to Birmingham, England, for months of ongoing treatment.

Malala Day

The attack on Malala sparked global outrage. While recovering she received calls of support, cards, and gifts from presidents, politicians, pop stars, and average people. In a video statement, Ziauddin thanked the well-wishers: "[Malala] wants me to tell everyone how grateful she is and is amazed that men, women and children from across the world are interested in her well-being."[2]

> "All I want is an education. And I am afraid of no one."[1]
>
> —Malala Yousafzai.

Three weeks after the shooting, the United Nations declared November 10 to be Malala Day. To commemorate the day, United Nations Special Envoy (and former British prime minister) Gordon Brown visited Pakistani president Asif Ali Zardari. Brown delivered a petition with more than 1 million signatures urging Zardari to make education available to all Pakistani children—both girls and boys. Brown pointed out that more than 60 million children worldwide do not attend school: "A world without school is a world without hope. We cannot all be a Malala Yousafzai, but we can all follow her, support her, pray for her."[3]

The Voice of 66 Million Girls

Since 2012 millions have followed and supported Malala as she became an activist—speaking out for the rights of girls and women throughout the world. In 2012 she was named one of *Time* magazine's 100 Most Influential People and was runner-up for the magazine's Person of the Year. On July 12, 2013, Malala's sixteenth birthday, she spoke before the United Nations, where she called for universal access to education.

Malala Yousafzai fearlessly defied the Taliban by speaking out about the importance of education for girls in her native Pakistan. In an effort to silence her, a Taliban gunman shot her in the head. Since her recovery, she has become a tireless advocate for education for young people worldwide.

Although she continued to receive death threats, Malala stated repeatedly that she was not interested in seeking revenge against the Taliban. She even advocates for educating girls who are daughters of Taliban members. And Malala remains fearless: "The terrorists thought they would change my aims and stop my ambitions, but nothing changed in my life except this: weakness, fear and hopelessness died. Strength, power and courage was born."[4]

In 2014, at age seventeen, Malala became the youngest person to ever receive the Nobel Peace Prize. Her Nobel speech summed up her beliefs: "Though I appear as one girl, one person, who is 5-foot-2-inches tall, if you include my high heels, I'm not a lone voice. I am those 66 million girls who are deprived of education and today I'm not raising my voice, it is the voice of those 66 million girls."[5]

She dedicated most of the Nobel Prize money to the Malala Fund to build schools in Pakistan and elsewhere. Despite the fact that she remains a target of the Taliban, Malala continues to bravely speak out for the right of all girls—and boys—everywhere to receive an education. She believes books and pens are the most powerful weapons of change.

> "A world without school is a world without hope."[3]
>
> —Gordon Brown, special envoy to the United Nations.

Chapter One

Born in a Conflicted Land

Malala Yousafzai was born on July 12, 1997, to mother Toor Pekai and father Ziauddin Yousafzai. Malala has two brothers, Khushal, born in 1999, and Atal, born in 2002. The Yousafzai family lived in Mingora, the only major city in the Swat Valley, a place where locals refer to themselves as Swatis.

Mingora is located in the rugged mountainous province of Khyber Pakhtunkhwa in Pakistan, on the Afghanistan border. With its towering mountain peaks, waterfalls, wildflowers, lakes, and emerald mines, the Swat Valley has long been a tourist destination. When Malala was born, Mingora was home to hotels, golf courses, and a famous bazaar that catered to tourists.

Members of the Yousafzai family are Sunni Muslim. They are also ethnic Pashtuns, members of an indigenous community composed of four major tribal confederacies. About 4 million Pashtuns live in the tribal region located on both sides of the Pakistan-Afghanistan border. About 30 million Pashtuns live outside this region in other parts of Afghanistan, Pakistan, and elsewhere.

The majority of people living in the Pashtun tribal region are extremely poor, with an average income of about $250 a year. Only 17 percent of the population can read and write—and most of those are men.

Roles of Men and Women

The governments of Pakistan and Afghanistan exert very little control over the tribal region. The law of the land is known as *Pashtunwali* (way of the Pashtuns). This code of behavior has guided the Pashtun people for more than twenty-five hundred years. Pashtuns who adhere to *Pashtunwali* are required to show profound respect to all visitors and to provide food and lodging. Pashtuns cannot turn away friends or relatives who come to visit, no matter how long they stay. When guests leave, hosts do not expect to be thanked; they understand that the guest is obligated to repay the hospitality at a later date.

The most important aspects of *Pashtunwali* revolve around revenge and honor, or *nang*. Malala writes of the importance of *nang*: "The worst thing that can happen to a Pashtun is loss of face. Shame is a very terrible thing for a Pashtun man."[6] Even a minor insult requires a violent response. If the person who expressed the insult is not available, the blood of his or her nearest male relative must be shed. This often leads to blood feuds that carry on for generations.

The roles of women in Pashtun society are governed by a concept called *purdah*, meaning "veiled" or "behind the curtain." *Purdah* establishes physical boundaries between women and men in order to protect a woman's honor. In many Pashtun homes, women have separate rooms for living and entertaining. Women who venture out in public are required to wear burkas (also spelled *burqas*). These garments cover the body from head to toe. Malala compares the burka to the cone-shaped birdies, or shuttlecocks, used in badminton: "Wearing a burqa is like walking inside [a] big fabric shuttlecock with only a grille to see through and on hot days it's like an oven."[7]

A Different Child

Although *purdah* is meant to honor women, Pashtun society gives males a higher status than females. When a boy is born, Pashtun men fire their rifles in the air in celebration. When a girl is born, there are no festivities; Pashtun girls are raised primarily to cook and clean. When they grow up they are expected to fulfill their duties by marrying and having children.

When Malala was born only one male cousin, Khan Yousafzai, came to celebrate her birth. Khan presented Malala's father with a drawing of the Yousafzai clan's large family tree. It showed only the male lineage going back three hundred years. When presented with the gift, Ziauddin picked up a pen, drew a line from his name, and wrote "Malala."

Malala Yousafzai's Birthplace: Mingora, Pakistan

Khan was shocked, but Ziauddin was different from most Pashtun men; he believed his daughter was a gift. He later said the minute he looked into Malala's eyes, he fell in love and told Khan: "I know there is something different about this child."[8] Ziauddin broke tradition in another way. He asked his friends to place dried fruits, candy, and coins in Malala's cradle, something normally only done for Pashtun boys.

In everyday life, Pashtuns only use their first names; family or tribal names are reserved for formal settings. Ziauddin named his daughter after a Pashtun folk hero, a young woman named Malalai of Maiwand. Malalai is credited with helping rally the Afghan army to defeat the British military, which occupied Maiwand in 1880. Ziauddin was proud of the name since it represented a strong Pashtun woman. Malala was thrilled with her name and the way her father remembered Malalai's heroic deeds: "I loved hearing the story and the songs my father sang to me, and the way my name floated on the wind when people called it."[9]

"A Born Teacher"

Ziauddin's attitudes were more liberal than those of most other Pashtuns, but this was not the result of a more liberal childhood. On the contrary, Ziauddin grew up in a traditional household that was dominated by his father, Rohul Amin Yousafzai. Ziauddin was born in 1969 in the small village of Shangla in the Swat Valley. His father owned several schools and was also an imam, or Muslim religious leader, known for giving mesmerizing speeches. Unlike his father, Ziauddin was not a gifted orator; in fact, he had a stuttering problem. Rohul had little patience for his son's stuttering and became angry when it took Ziauddin a minute or two to utter a single sentence. Although Ziauddin was tormented by his father and male cousins for his speech impediment, he loved words and poetry. He eventually overcame his problem by entering public speaking contests. Somehow, when giving a speech before a crowd, Ziauddin's stutter vanished. As a young man, he won first prize in several speaking competitions.

Ziauddin excelled in school. His father wanted him to study to become a doctor, but according to Ziauddin, "I was a born teacher and had a great passion for this profession right from a very early age. While I was an 8th grader I used to climb up a tall mountain to help my elder brother who was a teacher in a primary public school."[10]

At age eighteen Ziauddin attended Jahanzeb College in a beautiful mountain village called Spal Bandi. After receiving a master's degree in

> "I was a born teacher and had a great passion for this profession right from a very early age."[10]
>
> —Ziauddin Yousafzai, educator and father of Malala.

English, Ziauddin and a fellow student opened an English-language school for girls in Mingora; the school later expanded to include boys. Ziauddin and his partner used their savings to rent a two-story building with a walled courtyard. Ziauddin named the institution Khushal School. The name came from one of his heroes, Khushal Khan Khattak, a warrior-poet who lived in the seventeenth century.

> *"I strongly believe that for girls . . . education is . . . an emancipation. It is empowerment and independence."[11]*
>
> —Ziauddin Yousafzai, educator and father of Malala.

Although other schools had failed in Mingora, Ziauddin was motivated by the belief that all children—rich and poor, male and female—deserve an education. He also thought that Pakistan's widespread poverty and violence could be transformed into peace and prosperity through education. Ziauddin wanted to elevate the role of females in Pashtun society: "I strongly believe that for girls . . . education is not simply literacy and skill to earn. Rather, it is beyond that. It is an emancipation. It is empowerment and independence."[11]

Toor Pekai

Malala's mother, Toor Pekai, was also born in Shangla. She started school at age six but did not finish. Although she was the only girl at school, she attended every day. However, she envied her female cousins who got to stay home and play all day. One day she decided to drop out, so she sold her books and spent the money on sweets. Although Toor Pekai's father had encouraged her to attend school, he did not seem to notice when she stopped.

Malala describes her mother as very beautiful, with green eyes and chestnut brown hair. Her beauty attracted the attention of Ziauddin. Since men and women are not allowed to date in traditional Pashtun society, Ziauddin courted Toor Pekai by sending her love poems. At this time Toor Pekai began to regret her lack of education; she was illiterate and could not read Ziauddin's poetic words.

Toor Pekai and Ziauddin were married in 1995 just as Khushal School was about to open. Because Ziauddin had invested all his money in the school, the couple could not afford a traditional Pashtun wedding, which can involve several days of feasting. After their simple ceremony, Toor Pekai moved to Mingora, where she helped Ziauddin and his partner work to open the school. The couple moved into three rooms above the school, and Toor Pekai was pregnant within a few months. However, their first child, a girl, was stillborn.

Ziauddin expected to support Khushal School with the money students paid to attend, but attendance was low, and the school struggled to survive. At the time Malala was born in 1997, Ziauddin could not afford to hire many employees. He worked as teacher, principal, accountant, and janitor. The school had six teachers, including Ziauddin, and about one hundred pupils. Each student paid 100 rupees a month (about $2.50). However, all the money went toward paying the teachers and rent; there was little money left for buying food for Ziauddin's family.

Ziauddin (far left) and Toor Pekai (second from right) inspired in their three children (from left, Atal, Khushal, and Malala) a love for education. The family appears together in 2014 after Malala was named as winner of the Nobel Peace Prize.

Growing Up in School

As a child, Malala had no awareness of her family's financial predicament. She knew only that she loved living above her father's school. Even before she could talk, she toddled into classrooms and went to the front of the class to pretend she was a teacher. By the time she was four, Malala was attending classes for older children: "I used to sit in wonder, listening to everything they were being taught. Sometimes I would mimic the teachers. You could say I grew up in a school."[12]

By age seven Malala was at the top of her class, and she often tutored struggling classmates. She also participated in extracurricular activities, including drama, art, singing, badminton, and cricket. Although she excelled in the competitive school environment, Malala could not afford to buy nice things, because of her family's financial situation. This left her feeling very jealous of her friend Safina, who had many nice dolls and shoeboxes full of jewelry. So Malala decided to steal from Safina when she was studying at Safina's house. At first the theft provided Malala with a thrill, but soon it became a compulsion she could not stop. Malala hid the pilfered goods in boxes in her bedroom, but one afternoon she came home to find them gone. Her mother had found the items and returned them to Safina. Toor Pekai decided not to punish Malala, but she did tell her husband of their daughter's actions. Ziauddin was extremely disappointed; this only added to Malala's shame. Malala writes about how this event changed her life:

> Since that day I have never lied or stolen. Not a single lie nor a single penny, not even the coins my father leaves around the house, which we're allowed to buy snacks with. I also stopped wearing jewelry because I asked myself, What are these baubles which tempt me? Why should I lose my character for a few metal trinkets? But I still feel guilty, and to this day I say sorry to God in my prayers.[13]

After the theft incident, Malala worked extra hard to regain her parents' respect. When she saw a notice posted on the school wall for an upcoming public speaking contest, Malala decided to surprise her father by entering. The topic she was randomly assigned was even more surprising: Honesty is the best policy.

Malala's Namesake

Malala Yousafzai's namesake is Malalai of Maiwand. She was one of the greatest heroines in Pashtun culture. Born in 1861, Malalai was the daughter of shepherds who lived in Khig, near the town of Maiwand in southern Kandahar Province in Afghanistan. In 1880 Maiwand was occupied by British military forces attempting to colonize the region. Malalai's father and fiancé were members of the Afghan army fighting the British. Malalai, her mother, and other Pashtun women cared for the wounded Afghan soldiers and provided water and spare weapons to the troops.

Legend has it that the British were winning the battle when Malalai picked up the Afghan flag and shouted to her fiancé: "Young love! If you do not fall in the battle of Maiwand, By God, someone is saving you as a symbol of shame!" Malalai's cry provided the Afghan fighters with strengthened resolve, and they redoubled their efforts.

Malalai was soon killed by an enemy bullet. However, the Afghans were able to rout the British, who beat a disastrous retreat back to Kandahar. At the time the loss was one of the worst defeats in British military history. Malalai, who was about eighteen years old, was buried with honors in Khig, where her grave remains today.

Quoted in Garen Ewing, "The Second Anglo-Afghan War 1879–1880," Second Anglo-Afghan War, 2005. www.garenewing.co.uk.

In Pashtun culture, a public speech presented in a student contest is traditionally written by the speaker's father or uncle. Following this custom Ziauddin wrote Malala's speech. He used quotes from a letter attributed to Abraham Lincoln, written in the 1860s. In the letter Lincoln writes to his son's headmaster: "Teach him to learn to lose and also to enjoy winning. . . . Teach him it is far more honorable to fail than to cheat."[14]

On the day of the contest, Malala's father and grandfather were in attendance. She was so nervous she trembled with fear. While Malala read the speech she lost her place several times, struggling to read the paper with shaking hands. When the judges announced the results, Malala came in second place. But she took Lincoln's words to heart and learned from her loss. Malala also began writing her own speeches, using words that came from her heart.

Learning Compassion

One day in 2004 Malala was taking the household trash to a garbage dump for her mother when she noticed a young girl scavenging among the flies and rotting food. The girl had matted hair and her body was covered with sores. The girl was among a group of children picking cans, bottles, and paper from the mountain of rubbish to sell to neighborhood recyclers for a few rupees.

Malala ran home in tears and begged her father to offer the girl a free place in his school. Ziauddin wished he could, but Malala's mother had already convinced him to allow numerous girls to attend Khushal School for free. They included a cousin from another village that had no school and daughters of two women who helped Toor Pekai with housework. The girls were provided with more than education; Toor Pekai understood that children could not learn when they were hungry, so she cooked them all breakfast every morning.

By this time Khushal School's population had grown to eight hundred students; one hundred of them attended for free. Ziauddin's generosity cost him more than money; wealthy parents pulled their kids out of school when they saw their children sitting in classrooms with the children of servants. But Malala was still concerned about the young garbage picker, so Ziauddin decided to raise awareness about the problem. He printed up flyers with pictures of young scavengers under the headline "Is education not right for these children?"[15] He distributed the flyers at public meetings and left them in shops.

Politics at Her Father's Knee

Ziauddin posted the flyers because he wished to help the poor people of his region, but the military officials who ran Pakistan viewed the flyers as a threat. By his actions, Ziauddin was seen as publicly criticizing the government for its lack of interest in providing public educa-

In 2012 students gather outside Khushal School, opened and run by Ziauddin Yousafzai. Ziauddin has long believed that young people have a right to an education regardless of gender and economic circumstances.

tion to Pakistani children. A local military commander ominously said in public that Ziauddin posed a threat to public order.

Ziauddin was also condemned for speaking out about official corruption in the education system. In Pakistan it was common for officials to promise to open public schools in remote areas. After obtaining money for buildings and supplies, the officials simply kept the funds.

Ziauddin was also concerned about the environment. The people of Mingora had once breathed fresh mountain air. But by 2004 Mingora's population was about 175,000, and polluted air had become the norm thanks to the growing number of vehicles and cooking fires. The fires were fueled by the surrounding forests, which were being stripped of trees at an alarming rate. Additionally, only about half of Mingora's population had access to safe drinking water. And most families, including Malala's, relieved themselves outdoors since they had no indoor plumbing.

Malala later wrote that these problems could be solved with government money. But powerful military leaders and politicians were looting the country's treasury. Officials took out large loans from state banks and never repaid them. Bureaucrats required bribes to perform their jobs and directed lucrative contracts to family businesses. While Pakistanis suffered from power outages, polluted drinking water, and lack of public schools, politicians bought expensive homes in London.

These issues were among the many that sparked debate in Malala's home. As she recalls, her father's activism was inspirational: "From an early age I was interested in politics and sat on my father's knee listening to everything he and his friends discussed."[16]

War Comes to the Swat Valley

The most pressing problem to come to the Swat Valley was caused by events thousands of miles away. On September 11, 2001, terrorists affiliated with the group al Qaeda, who had trained in Afghanistan, hijacked passenger jets and flew them into the World Trade Center in New York City and the Pentagon in Washington, DC. Nearly three thousand people were killed. The Swat Valley residents had difficulty understanding the 9/11 terrorist attacks. The largest buildings in Mingora were the hospital and hotel, each only three stories high. As Malala writes: "I had no idea what New York and America were. The school was my world and my world was the school. We did not realize then that 9/11 would change our world too, and would bring war into our valley."[17]

> "From an early age I was interested in politics and sat on my father's knee listening to everything he and his friends discussed."[16]
>
> —Malala Yousafzai.

The terrorist attack led the United States to invade Afghanistan less than a month later, on October 7, 2001. The object of the mission was to destroy al Qaeda and capture Osama bin Laden, the group's leader. To defeat al Qaeda, the United States would also have to defeat the fundamentalist Taliban government that controlled Afghanistan. The United States defeated the Taliban and took control of Afghanistan within seventy-eight days. However, Bin Laden and several thousand al Qaeda and Taliban fighters escaped into the mountainous

A Girl's Life

In a 2014 speech in Vancouver, Canada, Ziauddin Yousafzai described life for Pashtun girls growing up in Pakistan and Afghanistan, where women's rights are severely limited by religion and ancient traditions:

> Right from the very beginning, when a girl is born, her birth is not celebrated. She is not welcomed, neither by father nor by mother. The neighborhood comes and commiserates with the mother, and nobody congratulates the father. And a mother is very uncomfortable for having a girl child. When she gives birth to the first girl child, first daughter, she is sad. When she gives birth to the second daughter, she is shocked, and in the expectation of a son, when she gives birth to a third daughter, she feels guilty like a criminal.

> Not only the mother suffers, but the daughter, the newly born daughter, when she grows old, she suffers too. At the age of five, while she should be going to school, she stays at home and her brothers are admitted in a school. . . . [When] she becomes 13 years old, she is forbidden to go out of her home without a male escort. She is confined under the four walls of her home.... A good girl is supposed to be very quiet, very humble and very submissive. It is the criteria. The role model good girl should be very quiet. She is supposed to be silent and she is supposed to accept the decisions of her father and mother and the decisions of elders, even if she does not like them.

Ziauddin Yousafzai, "My Daughter Malala," TED, March 2014. www.ted.com.

Pashtun tribal area of South Waziristan, Pakistan, about 300 miles (483 km) from Mingora.

By 2003 the Taliban had set up training camps in the tribal region and used them to conduct cross-border raids on US troops. The Taliban also engaged in numerous skirmishes with the Pakistani army. In

2004 the Pakistan government brokered a peace deal with the Taliban that gave the group control of the Swat Valley and nearby tribal areas. The Taliban, made up largely of Pashtuns, openly recruited young men to join the jihad, or struggle, against the invading US troops.

The United States began using unmanned aerial vehicles (UAVs), or drones, against the Taliban. In June 2004 for instance, a US drone strike targeted a group of Taliban leaders in South Waziristan. As drone attacks increased so did casualties; civilians were among those killed by US strikes. Outraged local clerics called on their followers to avenge the deaths by carrying out suicide bombing missions against Pakistani soldiers who were seen as allies of the United States.

> *"I had no idea what New York and America were. . . . We did not realize then that 9/11 would change our world too, and would bring war into our valley."[17]*
>
> —Malala Yousafzai.

Although the war was still far away from Mingora, Ziauddin feared that it was only a matter of time until the battle reached the Swat Valley. He urged local clerics to preach peace and stop encouraging the Taliban to build training camps in the area. Few listened. Ziauddin was only one voice, and there was nothing he could do to stop the inevitable violence threatening to engulf his family, his school, and his city.

Chapter Two

The Taliban Comes to Swat Valley

Malala Yousafzai was just ten years old in 2007 when the Taliban embarked on a campaign to control the Swat Valley. At the time she was reading the vampire fantasy books in Stephenie Meyer's Twilight series. Malala said the Taliban arrived in the night like vampires, but they were nothing like Twilight's handsome hero Edward Cullen. Malala says the heavily armed Taliban fighters looked more like beggars with their long beards and scraggly hair. They wore camouflage vests and traditional Afghan *shalwar kamiz*, which are pajama-like trousers and long tunics. Malala's impression at the time was that the soldiers desperately needed baths and barbers.

Swatis did not refer to the turban-wearing fighters as Taliban but as the Tor Patki, or the Black-Turbaned Brigade. The group was formally known as the Tehreek Nifaz-e-Shariat Mohammadi (TNSM), or Movement for the Enforcement of Islamic Law. If the group's motivation was not clear enough by its name, fighters also wore badges that clearly stated their aim: Sharia Law or Martyrdom. Members of the Taliban were willing to die for their cause.

The Radio Mullah

Some Taliban leaders called themselves mullahs, a term derived from the Arabic word meaning "master" or "guardian." Mullahs are generally recognized as experts on sharia law and the Quran, or Islamic holy book. However, most of the mullahs in the Taliban were barely literate. They had attended religious schools called madrassas, sponsored by fundamentalists in Saudi Arabia, where education consisted of little more than memorizing passages of the Quran. Ziauddin often complained that anyone can call himself a mullah and the title means nothing. As Malala explains: "Mullahs often misinterpret the Quran . . . when they teach it in our country as few people understand the original [text]."[18]

The leader of the Taliban in the Swat Valley, Mullah Fazlullah, was among those misinterpreting the Quran. The twenty-eight-year-old Fazlullah was far from a religious expert. He was well known to locals as the man who once operated the chairlift that carried people across the Swat River. As a childhood victim of polio, Fazlullah walked with a pronounced limp.

Despite his background, Fazlullah was able to take advantage of the fact that most Swatis were illiterate and too poor to afford televisions. Since radio was the main source of information, Fazlullah set up a pirate radio station. It broadcast from portable transmitters mounted on trucks and motor bikes. The station, which everyone seemed to listen to, aired daily for two hours in the morning and two hours in the evening. People began referring to the station as Mullah FM. As the main voice of Mullah FM, Fazlullah was known as the Radio Mullah. Malala describes the broadcasts:

In the beginning, Fazlullah was very wise. He introduced himself as an Islamic reformer and an interpreter of the Quran. . . . He used his station to encourage people to adopt good habits and abandon practices he said were bad. . . . Sometimes his voice was reasonable, like when adults are trying to persuade you to do something you don't want to do [but at other times] it was scary and full of fire. Often he would weep as he spoke of his love for Islam.[19]

Malala says that many women, including her devout mother, fell under the spell of the Radio Mullah. When he was off the air, he appeared as a romantic figure, riding from village to village on a black horse. Fazlullah's long hair blew in the wind, and his erect riding posture was compared to the Prophet Muhammad. According to Malala, "Lots of women were so moved by what Fazlullah said that they gave him gold and money . . . particularly in poor villages or households where the husband was working abroad. . . . Some gave their life savings, believing this would make God happy."[20]

Taliban Edicts

In his broadcasts Fazlullah spoke for hours about gender roles under sharia law. Sometimes he ordered all male listeners to go outside while he spoke exclusively to women. Malala describes Fazlullah's message: "Women are meant to fulfill their responsibilities in the home. Only in emergencies can they go outside, but they must wear their veil."[21] By veils, Fazlullah meant burkas. Women who violated this edict could be flogged, and those who engaged in extramarital sex or committed other sins might be shot, hung, or beheaded. The Taliban also instituted rules for men, although these rules were not nearly as harsh. Men were required to wear head coverings and *shalwar kamiz*. Long beards were

An armed member of the Pakistani Taliban patrols the Swat Valley in 2009. The Taliban imposed their extreme and stringent interpretation of Islam on the people of the region.

Taliban Madrassas

The Taliban has Pashtun roots, but many of its members attended free religious schools called madrassas. The schools were supported by Islamic fundamentalists in Saudi Arabia. Madrassas, which remain numerous in Afghanistan and Pakistan, teach an austere form of Arab Islam called Wahhabism. Madrassas attract the poor; in some regions of Pakistan they are the only schools available.

Mullah Fazlullah, leader of the Pakistani Taliban, was a product of madrassa schooling. Fazlullah had studied in a madrassa run by Sufi Mohammad, the founder of the Taliban group TNSM. When Sufi Mohammad was imprisoned in 2002, Fazlullah married his daughter and took over the TNSM. Shaista Wahab, an Afghan history professor at the University of Nebraska, describes madrassa education: "The curriculum of the madrassas was based on repetition of the Qur'an and a handful of other texts and [imparted] the simple messianic, puritan values of an imagined primitive Islam. The mullahs who ran the schools often confused Pashtun custom with Islamic law, especially in matters of gender roles."

Shaista Wahab, *A Brief History of Afghanistan*. New York: Infobase, 2007, p. 205.

compulsory. Those who trimmed their beards or shaved were subject to ten days in prison.

The Taliban also had a harsh view of art and music. Its views are based on extreme interpretations of the Prophet Muhammad's teachings. The Taliban preaches that it is sinful to create a visual representation of any living creature. In practice, this belief led to a ban on videos, movies, television, photography, and painting. Even sculptures, including the ancient statutes found in the Swat museum, were forbidden. Music also has no place in the world of the Taliban. The group banned musical instruments, records, cassettes, CDs, and music players. Radio was also banned, except Mullah FM, which played no music. Malala describes how this edict affected life in Mingora: "People were getting rid of their TVs, DVDs and CDs. Fazlullah's men collected them into huge heaps on the streets and set them on fire, creating clouds of thick black smoke that reached high into the sky. Hundreds of CD and DVD shops closed."[22]

Malala and her brothers loved watching television and DVDs and continued to do so. However, they were forced to take extreme precautions. The Taliban had created a morality police force called the Falcon Commandos. Members patrolled the streets in pickup trucks with mounted machine guns and harassed anyone said to be violating sharia law. At night the commandos would go from house to house and listen at people's doors. If they heard a television playing, they would break down the door, grab the set, and smash it to pieces in the street. This prompted Ziauddin to move the family television into a cupboard; Malala and her younger brothers could only watch with the volume turned very low.

The commandos even rampaged against children's board games. If they heard children laughing, they would burst into the room and smash whatever games they found. Malala wrote about the situation: "We felt like the Taliban saw us as little dolls to control, telling us what to do and how to dress. I thought if God wanted us to be like that He wouldn't have made us all different."[23]

Brutality

The Taliban tightened its control through terror, publicly flogging anyone found guilty in sharia courts. Among those whipped were teenage girls caught without burkas. As hundreds of people watched, the crowd yelled *Allah Akbar*," or "God is great," after each lash. Although flogging was a common punishment in Saudi Arabia, the gruesome public displays had never before been seen in the Swat Valley.

The Taliban introduced another brutal practice: kidnapping and killing political activists and prosperous businessmen. Malala's family was among those who attracted the attention of the Taliban. One day a note for Ziauddin was tacked to the door of Khushal School: "Sir, the school you are running is Western and infidel. You teach girls and have a uniform that is un-Islamic. Stop this or you will be in trouble and your children will weep and cry for you."[24] The note was signed, "Fedayeen of Islam." (*Fedayeen* is an Arabic term for someone who gives his life for a cause.)

To safeguard his students, Ziauddin changed the boy's school uniform from Western-style pants and shirt to *shalwar kamiz*. Girls were instructed to wear white head scarfs and keep their heads covered when walking to and from school. But Ziauddin was not about to close the school. He wrote a letter to the local paper pointing out that the Fedayeen and the children all prayed to the same God. Ziauddin said that members of the Taliban could kill him if they wished, but he asked them to please spare the lives of his students.

The First Battle of Swat

In October 2007 the Taliban continued to consolidate its power in the Swat Valley, overrunning at least fifty-nine villages and always using the same tactics: Fazlullah's men entered a town and attacked the local police station. The overwhelmed police were killed. Those who managed to escape either quit the force or joined the Taliban to avoid assassination. Malala felt her whole country had gone crazy since no one resisted or protested when the black-and-white TNSM flag was hoisted over their villages.

> "Sir, the school you are running is Western and infidel. You teach girls and have a uniform that is un-Islamic. Stop this or you will be in trouble and your children will weep and cry for you."[24]
>
> —Fedayeen of Islam, a Taliban leader.

Up to this point, the Pakistani military had largely ignored the actions of the Taliban. However, the government now feared that the Taliban was gaining enough strength to capture Islamabad, the Pakistani capital. On October 24, about three thousand Pakistani troops swept into the Swat Valley to launch what is now known as the First Battle of Swat. At that time helicopters were a rare sight in Swat. When the noisy aircraft rumbled over Mingora for the first time, Malala and her schoolmates excitedly ran outside to wave at the airborne soldiers. But the exhilaration turned to distress the next day when the army began its pursuit of Fazlullah and his Taliban fighters, who had escaped to the rugged mountains surrounding Mingora. In the weeks that followed, cannons and machine guns echoed in the hills all night long. Malala, her family, and everyone else in Mingora found it difficult to sleep.

The number of Pakistani troops would grow to fifteen thousand by mid-November, and according to Malala, Mingora began to resemble more of a military base than a city. However, the outnumbered Taliban managed to maintain control over a large portion of the Swat Valley outside Mingora. Fierce fighting continued until the end of December, when winter conditions halted the fighting. But even as twelve thousand troops set up permanent camps in Mingora, about 70 percent of the valley remained in Taliban control. And Fazlullah continued with the daily Radio Mullah broadcasts throughout 2008.

A Wave of Terror

The army presence only seemed to make things worse for the civilian inhabitants of the Swat Valley. Malala recalls that the Taliban blended into the local population, and Fazlullah used his broadcasts to encourage suicide bombers to kill Pakistani soldiers and civilians who worked

Local residents look at the ruins of a girls' school, one of dozens of schools destroyed in a Taliban terror campaign in the Swat Valley beginning in 2008. Malala's father publicly challenged these and other actions of the Taliban, describing the group's activities as un-Islamic.

The Power of Women

The Taliban leader Mullah Fazlullah often stated that girls and women had no power and should always remain subservient to men. As Malala Yousafzai writes, she was confused by these words:

> In our Islamic studies class at school we used to write essays entitled "How the Prophet Lived." We learned that the first wife of the Prophet [Muhammad] was a businesswoman called Khadijah. She was forty, fifteen years older than him, and she had been married before, yet he still married her. I also knew from watching my own mother that Pashtun women are very powerful and strong. Her mother, my grandmother, had looked after all eight children alone after my grandfather had an accident and broke his pelvis and could not leave his bed for eight years.
>
> A man goes out to work, he earns a wage, he comes back home, he eats, he sleeps. That's what he does. Our men think earning money and ordering around others is where power lies. They don't think power is in the hands of the woman who takes care of everyone all day long, and gives birth to their children. In our house my mother managed everything because my father was so busy. It was my mother who would wake up early in the morning, iron our school clothes, make our breakfast and teach us how to behave. It was my mother who would go to the market, shop for us and cook. All those things she did.

Malala Yousafzai and Christina Lamb, *I Am Malala: The Story of the Girl Who Stood Up for Education and Was Shot by the Taliban.* London: Weidenfeld & Nicolson, 2013, p. 116.

with the government. Fazlullah also encouraged his men to blow up girls' schools because they were forbidden under sharia law. A girls' primary school in Matta, about 20 miles (32 km) from Mingora, was the first to be destroyed. Soon the bombing of girls' schools became a daily occurrence in the Swat Valley.

Malala's school was not bombed, but other blasts occurred in her neighborhood. One nearby blast, which shook Malala's house, was caused by a suicide bomber who blew himself up at the funeral of a local police chief who was also killed by a suicide bomber. Fifty-five mourners were killed, including women and young children. The daily carnage made Malala change her mind about the future. She had once planned to be a doctor but now wanted to be an inventor so she could create an anti-Taliban machine that would find and destroy the group's guns and bombs.

A Bright, Shining Young Lady

Ziauddin did not sit idly by as the violence increased. He joined the Swat Council of Elders, which was formed to challenge the Taliban. Since he could speak Pashto, English, and Urdu, the national language of Pakistan, Ziauddin was chosen as spokesperson for the council. In this role he often spoke to the media, challenging the Taliban and pointing out that its actions were un-Islamic.

When the council met at Ziauddin's home, Malala attended the meetings and listened quietly to the discussions. In June 2008, when she was only eleven years old, Malala began speaking to various media outlets. Her first interview was on ATV Khyber, the only Pashtun television channel. Malala explained that many girls had dropped out of school because of threats made by the Taliban. (Malala was allowed to appear on the program because she was not yet thirteen, the age when Pashto girls are obliged to observe *purdah*.)

Soon after her first interview, Malala appeared on GEO, the biggest news channel in Pakistan. The journalist who spoke with Malala referred to her as a shining example of a bright young lady and told her she was wise

> *"You are a child and it's your right to speak."*[25]
>
> —Ziauddin Yousafzai, educator and father of Malala Yousafzai.

beyond her years. After the interview, Malala had much to think about: "The media needs interviews. They want to interview a small girl, but the girls are scared, and even if they're not, their parents won't allow it. I have a father who isn't scared, who stands by me. He said, 'You are a child and it's your right to speak.' . . . If one man, Fazlullah, can destroy everything, why can't one girl change it?"[25] Malala prayed every night for strength and courage as she continued to give interviews. When she appeared with Ziauddin on a talk show on BBC Urdu, Malala defiantly asked: "How dare the Taliban take away my basic right to education?"[26] After the interview, as reporters congratulated Malala, Ziauddin laughed and told his daughter she should go into politics.

A Reign of Terror

Malala felt her words were nothing more than blossoms blowing away in the wind as the destruction continued. By December 2008 the Taliban had turned more than four hundred girls' and boys' schools to rubble. They also blew up power stations and gas lines, leaving Malala and her neighbors without electricity or cooking gas. As bad as this was, things were about to get worse. At the end of 2008 Fazlullah announced that all girls' schools would have to close by January 15, 2009.

Ziauddin defied the Taliban order, vowing to keep his school open as long as any of his students and teachers were left alive. In her own way, Malala also defied their edict: She never once considered quitting school. She felt that education was her future and that the Taliban could take away her pens, paper, and school building but could never stop her from thinking.

Meanwhile, the Taliban continued with its reign of terror. Homes were bombed, policemen were beheaded, women were whipped, and teachers, musicians, and dancers were shot. The bodies were dumped every night in a central park that came to be called Bloody Square. To support its bloody deeds, the Taliban went door to door demanding money to buy guns. It also kidnapped boys and forced them to join the movement. Ziauddin personally received numerous death threats but kept them secret from his family.

Malala Becomes Gul Makai

In early January 2009 BBC radio correspondent Abdul Hai Kakkar contacted Ziauddin. Abdul asked whether Ziauddin knew a student who could write a blog called *The Diary of a Pakistani Schoolgirl*, which would describe life under the Taliban. Although Malala had never written a blog, she was quick to volunteer. At first Kakkar coached

Malala, asking her questions about her day, her conversations, and her dreams.

Since it was too dangerous to use her real name, Malala blogged under the pseudonym Gul Makai, a heroine from a Pashtun folktale. Her first blog appeared on January 3 under the heading "I Am Afraid." In it Malala described a recent nightmare and her fears of the Taliban: "I had a terrible dream yesterday with military helicopters and the Taliban. I have had such dreams since the launch of the military operation in Swat. My mother made me breakfast and I went off to school. I was afraid going to school because the Taliban had issued an edict banning all girls from attending schools."[27]

Malala also described the fears she felt while walking to school; she constantly looked over her shoulder for assassins. She wrote that school was the center of her life, but she was saddened that she could no longer wear her beloved royal-blue school uniform. Instead, she dressed in plain clothes and hid her books under her shawl so she would not attract attention from the Taliban.

Malala remained anonymous, but her blog attracted a great deal of attention, first from other students at her school and then far beyond the Swat Valley. Newspapers all over the world printed extracts from the blog, and the BBC used a voice actress to read blog excerpts on the air. Malala describes her reaction: "I began to see that the pen and the words that come from it can be much more powerful than machine guns, tanks or helicopters. We were learning how to struggle. And we were learning how powerful we are when we speak."[28]

> *"I began to see that the pen and the words that come from it can be much more powerful than machine guns, tanks or helicopters."*[28]
>
> —Malala Yousafzai.

A Request to the World

Malala might have felt empowered, but the teachers and students at her school were terrified. One teacher quit after he saw a beheaded corpse left near his home as a warning. And seventeen girls in Malala's class of twenty-seven stopped coming to school. While others hid, Malala suddenly became a video star.

On January 14, the day before the school closing deadline, a video journalist for the *New York Times* named Adam Ellick arrived at Malala's home with a camera. Ellick had heard of the eleven-year-old Pashtun blogger and convinced Ziauddin to let him make a documentary about the last day of operations at his girls' school. Ellick followed Malala throughout the day as she brushed her teeth, went to school, and hugged her friends good-bye after class. The documentary showed the school doors closing for the last time and included a statement from Malala: "They cannot stop me. I will get my education if it's at home, school or somewhere else. This is our request to the world—to save our schools, save our Pakistan, save our Swat."[29]

Despite her brave words, when Malala went home, she could not stop crying. She felt that when her school closed, she had lost one of the most important things in her life. Malala was also saddened when the BBC discontinued her blog on January 15 as Khushal School shut down.

A Peace Agreement

To everyone's surprise, the schools did not stay closed for long. In early February 2009, under intense pressure from the government and the media, Fazlullah agreed to lift the education ban for girls up to ten years old. Malala and some of the other girls who were older than ten also went back to school.

About a week later Swatis received what seemed like more welcome news: The Taliban and the government had reached a peace agreement. The agreement required the government to impose sharia law throughout the Swat Valley and the Taliban to stop fighting. It also allowed girls to return to school as long as those over age thirteen wore burkas.

The war had taken more than one thousand civilian lives and destroyed bridges, power plants, schools, and countless businesses. People had lived in a constant state of fear, but now an end to the fighting seemed near. Along with thousands of others, Malala and her family celebrated. However, Pakistan's allies in the United States were not happy with the deal, since the government would enforce sharia law. As Secretary of State Hillary Clinton announced: "I think the Pakistan government is basically abdicating [surrendering] to the Taliban and the extremists."[30]

Heeding evacuation orders issued by Pakistani authorities in May 2009, residents of Mingora await transport out of the Swat Valley. Like their neighbors, the Yousafzai family fled to a safer location until they were allowed to return home.

War Returns

Clinton's words turned out to be true. The Taliban took the peace agreement to mean that the TNSM was now officially sanctioned by the state. Taliban members continued to patrol the streets and harass women who were not wearing burkas. Additionally, the Taliban was gaining new ground. In April 2009 the group took over the Buner District, only 65 miles (105 km) from Islamabad.

The Taliban advances alarmed US president Barack Obama; Pakistan possessed more than two hundred nuclear bombs, and there were fears that the weapons might fall into Taliban hands. Under pressure from the United States, the Pakistani government launched a second attempt to destroy the Taliban. At the beginning of May, the Pakistani army ordered all civilians to leave Mingora. Malala said that leaving her home felt a lot like having her heart ripped out. Along with 2 million other people who had been forced to leave the Swat Valley, Malala and her family were officially classified as internally displaced persons.

Malala was more fortunate than most; her parents had relatives in their ancestral town, Shangla, where they could stay for a time. After three months they were allowed to return home; the Pakistani army had defeated the Taliban in Mingora after weeks of house-to-house fighting. The return was bittersweet. Nearly every building was pock-marked with bullet holes, and the streets were littered with blown-up buildings and rubble. The Yousafzai family was lucky; many homes in their neighborhood had been looted, but their rented home remained intact. Malala found to her joy that her school backpack, filled with textbooks, was where she had left it in her bedroom. Malala was now twelve years old and was thrilled to think she could go back to school and continue her education.

Chapter Three

Shot for Going to School

By the time Malala turned fourteen in July 2011, she was well known worldwide as an outspoken advocate for childhood education. In addition to granting numerous media interviews, Malala wrote essays for Open Minds Pakistan. This organization, run by a British group called the Institute for War & Peace Reporting, provides journalism training to teens and preteens. Malala also took on a political role as one of eleven girls in a group of sixty students that formed the District Child Assembly Swat, run by the charity UNICEF. Malala's peers elected her speaker, and together they passed resolutions, including an appeal for free schooling for disabled street children, an end to child labor, and reconstruction of schools destroyed by the Taliban.

International Recognition

More international recognition came Malala's way in October 2011 as one of five nominees for the international peace prize awarded by KidsRights, a children's advocacy group in Amsterdam, Netherlands. Although Malala did not win, she was thrilled by the recognition. Soon after, Malala was honored at home. She was invited to speak in Lahore at a fund-raising event for Daanish Schools, a network of new schools to be built for impoverished youth. At the Daanish Schools event, Malala was presented with a check for half a million rupees (about $4,500) to honor her outspoken promotion of girls' rights.

In her acceptance speech, Malala spoke publicly for the first time about her struggle to attend school in defiance of the Taliban edict against education for girls: "I know the importance of education because my pens and books were taken from me by force. But the girls of Swat are not afraid of anyone. We have continued with our education."[31]

Malala's stature continued to grow—both at home and abroad. In December 2011 she was awarded Pakistan's first-ever National Peace Prize. When news got out, Khushal School filled with journalists eager to conduct interviews. On December 20 Malala attended the award ceremony at the official residence of Yousaf Raza Gilani, the prime minister of Pakistan. In a speech, Gilani announced that the National Peace Prize would be renamed the Malala Prize and awarded annually to children under age eighteen. Although the setting was intimidating, Malala presented Gilani with a long list of demands after she was given the award and a check for a half-million rupees. Malala once again requested that all girls' schools be rebuilt and also demanded construction of a girls' university in the Swat Valley. As Malala expected, Gilani did not take her seriously. His reaction reinforced her dream of becoming a politician so she could one day accomplish the goals herself.

> "I know the importance of education because my pens and books were taken from me by force. But the girls of Swat are not afraid of anyone. We have continued with our education."[31]
>
> —Malala Yousafzai.

Awards and Prize Money

Despite their pride in her achievements, Malala's parents worried about the public recognition she was receiving. Pashtuns have a belief that people should only be honored when they are dead. To be honored while still alive is seen as a bad omen. As Toor Pekai stated: "I don't want awards, I want my daughter. I wouldn't exchange a single eyelash of my daughter for the whole world."[32] Ziauddin did not feel this way. He believed education was the only way to save Pakistan from corrupt politicians and the Taliban; he admired his daughter's willingness to speak out.

Malala continued to collect awards and checks. A local military leader gave Malala 100,000 rupees, and she used the money to build a science lab and library for Khushal School. Ziauddin used the rest of the money to buy Malala a bed and cabinet, pay for dental work for

Prime Minister Yousaf Raza Gilani of Pakistan awards the National Peace Prize to Malala Yousafzai in December 2011. At the award ceremony, Malala gave the prime minister a list of demands; among them were demands for rebuilding girls' schools and construction of a girls' university.

Toor Pekai, and buy a small piece of land in Shangla. The rest of Malala's prize money was spent on those who needed help the most. Ever since 2004, when Malala encountered a young girl scavenging for food in a mountain of garbage, the image had haunted her. She decided to make schooling for street children a priority and organized a group of twenty-one girls to start an educational foundation for the poor.

Ominous Threats

Malala's public profile increased in January 2012 when a girls' school in Karachi was named after her. Malala had never been to Karachi, which has a population of more than 20 million people. To attend the naming ceremony, she and her parents took a two-hour flight from Mingora. It was the first time Malala had ever flown on an airplane.

> "I don't want awards, I want my daughter. I wouldn't exchange a single eyelash of my daughter for the whole world."[32]
>
> —Toor Pekai Yousafzai, Malala's mother.

While in Karachi, Malala was visited by an American-based Pakistani journalist who had seen the 2009 documentary about Malala and the Khushal School closing, which had been posted on the *New York Times* website. The journalist alerted the Yousafzai family that the Taliban had that day issued a threat against Malala's life. The Taliban decreed that Malala should be killed for promoting the education of girls, which it viewed as a secular (nonreligious) and therefore unacceptable practice.

At first Malala did not take the warning seriously; as a regular user of the Internet, she had seen dozens of death threats posted on various social media sites. However, the next day Ziauddin was contacted by the Mingora police, who had heard the news and saw it as a serious threat. When Ziauddin suggested Malala keep a lower profile for a time, she refused. She later explained: "I don't know why, but hearing I was being targeted did not worry me. It seemed to me that everyone knows they will die one day. My feeling was that nobody can stop death; it doesn't matter if it comes from a *talib* [member of the Taliban] or cancer. So I should do whatever I want to do."[33]

When Malala returned to Mingora, the police offered to provide security guards, but she did not see the point of this. Powerful Pakistani politicians and others who had hired bodyguards for themselves had been killed by the Taliban despite the extra security. Malala resisted having bodyguards because she believed the presence of armed men would frighten her classmates and stop them from attending school.

Another threat arrived, this one against the school. An anonymous flier had appeared in all the local shops. It claimed Khushal School was the center of obscenity because it allowed the girls to stay at a

A Taliban Death Notice

In April 2012 Malala and her classmates celebrated completing their annual exams with a field trip to a beautiful green valley called Marghazar. The girls stayed in the luxurious White Palace hotel, went hiking, and had a picnic. When the girls returned home, they found an ominous Taliban flier that been had distributed to shopkeepers throughout Mingora. The notice, printed below, accused the girls of committing obscenities and falsely said Khushal School was run by a nongovernmental organization, or NGO. In parentheses, Malala adds her own clarification on this last point:

Dear Muslim brothers,

There is a school, the Khushal School, which is run by an NGO (NGOs have a very bad reputation among religious people in our country so this was a way to invite people's wrath) and is a center of vulgarity and obscenity. It is a Hadith [saying] of the Holy Prophet that if you see something bad or evil you should stop it with your own hand. If you are unable to do that then you should tell others about it, and if you can't do that you should think about how bad it is in your heart. I have no personal quarrel with the principal but I am telling you what Islam says. This school is a center of vulgarity and obscenity and they take girls for picnics to different resorts. If you don't stop it you will have to answer to God on Doomsday.

Quoted in Malala Yousafzai, "Malala Yousafzai (Ages 14–16)," 2015. http://malalacp.weebly.com.

motel while on a field trip. Although the notice did not explicitly call for violence against the school, it told readers that they would have to answer to God if they did not stop the vulgarity. Although most shopkeepers tossed the flier in the trash, it appeared on giant posters pasted to every mosque in the area. Malala's classmates were terrified.

Nightmares

Ziauddin was also frightened by this threat. His fears grew on August 3, 2012, when a close friend, Zahid Khan, was shot and seriously wounded while walking to the mosque near his home. Zahid was targeted for his membership in an activist group, the Global Peace Council. The group had been founded by Ziauddin to promote peace and education among local people. Fearing he might be targeted next by the Taliban, Ziauddin began exercising extreme caution when traveling, changing his route every day when going to and from school. But that was his only concession; he would not stop holding peace and education conferences.

Malala was also forced to take new precautions. She had turned fifteen in July and was considered an adult in the eyes of Islam. If the Taliban killed her now, it would not be accused of murdering a child, an act that was forbidden. Malala stopped walking the short distance to school and rode on a van-like school bus. At night while the family slept, Malala became compulsively vigilant. She walked the house, repeatedly checking to ensure that doors, windows, and outdoor gates were securely locked. Some nights she spent hours alternately praying and peering from her second-floor window. When sleep did come, Malala often had nightmares in which Taliban members would leap out at her with guns or bombs.

Shot on the Bus

With October exams approaching, Malala was nearly as concerned about school as she was about the Taliban threats. The night before her Pakistan Studies exam, Malala stayed up very late rereading her textbooks. The next day, October 9, 2012, the exam went better than expected. Afterward Malala felt energized, chatting with her friends while boarding the large van which served as her school bus. The vehicle had rows of bench seats and Malala sat down near the back of the van. Malala's brother Atal usually came over from his school to ride home with his sister, but decided to walk home with some of his friends that day.

As the bus took off, some of the girls were singing as Malala drummed a rhythm with her fingers on the seat. At that time of day the road was a colorful mix of city life. Malala saw a man butchering chickens in a market stall, chopping the heads off as blood dripped into the street. She remembers thinking, "Chop, chop, chop. Drip, drip, drip."[34] The air smelled of diesel exhaust, rubbish, and meat kebobs grilling on open fires.

The bus stopped at a routine army checkpoint and then resumed its journey. Malala did not see the two young Taliban members who stepped into the road and ordered the school bus to halt. She does not remember hearing a gunman shout: "Who is Malala?"[35] (No one answered, but several girls looked over at Malala, inadvertently signaling the gunman.) Malala picks up the story: "The last thing I remember is that I was thinking about the revision I needed to do for the next day [on an essay paper]. The sounds in my head were not the crack, crack, crack of three bullets, but the chop, chop, chop, drip, drip, drip of the man severing the heads of chickens, and them dropping into the dirty street, one by one."[36]

Emergency hospital staff tend to Malala after she was shot in the head on her ride home from school on October 9, 2012. The bullet missed her brain but dislodged bone fragments on the inside of her skull, causing life-threatening bleeding and swelling in the brain.

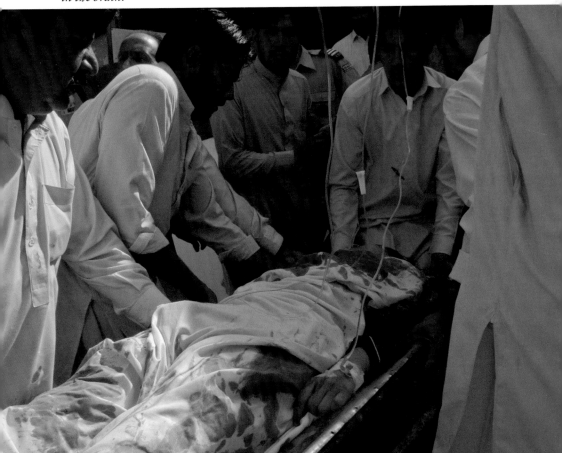

The Taliban bullet shot at point-blank range did not kill Malala but caused serious damage. The bullet entered her head above her left eye, passed along the outside of her skull and moved down her jaw-bone to her neck where it stopped, buried in muscle on her left shoulder. Malala slumped forward as two other bullets were fired. The second bullet hit Shazia Ramzan in the palm, and the third went through Shazia's collarbone, left her body, and grazed the right arm of Kainat Riaz. Malala's attackers ran from the bus as the driver sped to the nearest hospital. Blood was everywhere. One girl felt Malala's pulse and screamed that she was still alive.

A Swelling Brain

News of the attack spread quickly through Mingora. Ziauddin learned what had happened as he was about to make an important presentation to four hundred Swati school principals. He hurriedly gave his speech before rushing to the Saidu Sharif Medical Complex where Malala had been taken. When he arrived Ziauddin had to push through a crowd of reporters, photographers, and TV cameramen. He found Malala lying on a stretcher with a bandage over her head, and he kissed her face repeatedly and told her she was brave and he loved her. Someone said Malala smiled. Her words describe his pain:

> Seeing me like that was the worst thing that had ever happened to him. All children are special to their parents, but to my father I was his universe. I had been his comrade in arms for so long, first secretly as Gul Makai, then quite openly as Malala. He had always believed that if the Taliban came for anyone, it would be for him, not me. He said he felt as if he had been hit by a thunderbolt.[37]

Doctors ran a CAT scan on Malala, which takes a series of X-rays from different angles and provides cross-section images of the body. The CAT scan showed the bullet had miraculously missed Malala's brain. However, the bullet's impact had dislodged bone fragments on the inside of her skull, causing bleeding and swelling in the brain—a life-threatening condition. A portion of Malala's skull needed to be removed to make room for the swelling, but the medical center was not equipped to perform this delicate operation.

At 3:00 p.m., about three hours after the shooting, a Pakistani military commander ordered an army helicopter to take Malala and Ziauddin to the provincial capital, Peshawar, where military doctors could perform the surgery. On the short ambulance ride to the heliport, Ziauddin was terrified that the Taliban would attack his daughter again.

By this time the Taliban had taken credit for the attack, but the group claimed Malala was not targeted for her education campaign. The Taliban said Malala was shot for preaching secularism and Western values and for praising Barack Obama when asked by an interviewer to name her favorite politician. As Taliban spokesman Ehsanullah Ehsan stated in a phone message to reporters: "[Malala] was pro-West, she was speaking against the Taliban and she was calling President Obama her idol. She was young but she was promoting Western culture in Pashtun areas."[38] The spokesman also noted that the attack had been ordered in August by Mullah Fazlullah and that anyone who opposed the Taliban or sided with the government could expect the same treatment.

> "[Malala] was pro-West, she was speaking against the Taliban and she was calling President Obama her idol. She was young but she was promoting Western culture in Pashtun areas."[38]
>
> —Ehsanullah Ehsan, Taliban spokesman.

A Delicate Operation

Malala was flown to Peshawar without incident. She was conscious but not speaking or alert when she was rushed to the intensive care unit at the Combined Military Hospital. Doctors took another CAT scan from a different angle, and it showed Malala was more seriously wounded than previously believed. Bone fragments had damaged the outer membrane that encloses the brain. Doctors felt Malala could not survive an operation to remove the bullet in her neck at that time. She was put in a hospital bed and closely monitored.

Toor Pekai and Malala's brothers arrived by car at the hospital in Peshawar about four hours after Malala. The family gathered around

"Disgusting and Tragic"

When Malala was shot, people all over the world expressed outrage and prayed for her recovery. Free medical treatment was offered by government officials in the United States, Germany, Singapore, and Great Britain. At the United Nations, Secretary General Ban Ki-moon called the attack heinous and cowardly. In a Washington, DC, briefing, Barack Obama's press secretary, Jay Carney, addressed the attack: "I know that the President found the news reprehensible and disgusting and tragic. We strongly condemn the shooting of Malala Yousafzai. . . . Directing violence at children is barbaric, it's cowardly. And our hearts go out to her and the others who were wounded, as well as their families. The United States has offered any necessary assistance to Malala."

Jay Carney, "Press Briefing by Press Secretary Jay Carney, 10/10/2012," White House, October 10, 2012. www.whitehouse.gov.

Malala's bed, weeping and praying. By this time, dozens of politicians, government ministers, and military officials were gathered in the hospital waiting room. Malala's face was on every television channel as news of the shooting traveled around the world.

Around midnight, Malala's condition worsened. Her brain was swelling dangerously, and she was fading in and out of consciousness. Doctors began operating around 1:30 a.m., using a surgical saw to remove a piece of bone from the left part of her skull. The bone fragment was placed into the tissue under the skin of Malala's abdomen to preserve it. Doctors planned to put it back in three months after the swelling went down. Blood clots were removed from Malala's brain, and the bullet was removed from her shoulder.

Dawn was breaking by the time the doctors finished. The operation was a success, but Malala had to be placed in a medically induced coma. This type of coma is used to prevent brain swelling by reducing the rate of blood flow to the brain.

"A Child Alive"

That afternoon Malala was visited by Javid Kayani and Fiona Reynolds, two doctors from Birmingham, England, who happened to be in the region. Kayani is an emergency care consultant, and Reynolds is a specialist in children's intensive care. The British doctors were alarmed by the care Malala was receiving. When patients are in medically induced comas, their critical life functions need to be monitored constantly. But the hospital was not closely watching Malala's blood pressure, oxygen levels, and other vital signs. The British doctors believed Malala's chances for recovery were being compromised. However, because of other commitments, they were unable to stay with her.

By October 11 Malala was nearing death. Her blood was not clotting, her blood pressure was very low, and her kidneys were failing. Reynolds was on her way to the airport to return to Birmingham when she heard news of Malala's condition. She turned around and went to the hospital with two British nurses. Although Malala was very ill, Reynolds arranged for her to be transported to a helipad and airlifted to the Armed Forces Institute of Cardiology, a better-equipped hospital in Rawalpindi, a seventy-five-minute flight from Peshawar.

Reynolds performed heroically under difficult conditions. Peshawar was extremely dangerous for foreigners, and there were fears the Taliban might shoot up the ambulance or try to bring down the helicopter with a rocket. But Reynolds later said the risk was worth it: "There is now a child alive who could make a lot of difference to the world."[39]

> "There is now a child alive who could make a lot of difference to the world."[39]
>
> —Fiona Reynolds, Malala's doctor.

When Malala arrived, the hospital was put on complete lockdown to guard against another attempt on her life. A battalion of soldiers stood around the building, and snipers were stationed on the roof. No one could enter or leave the grounds, and all mobile phones were confiscated for security reasons. After three hours of intense work, Reynolds managed to stabilize Malala's condition. During this period, Kayani worked to convince Pakistani military leaders to allow Malala to be flown to England. Without extensive rehabilitation she would have a speech impediment and a weak right arm and leg. Time was short; she needed to be moved within two or three days.

After hours of negotiation, officials agreed to allow Malala to leave Pakistan. She was transported on October 15 to the Queen Elizabeth Hospital in Birmingham, England. When Malala's parents heard the news, they were distraught. Malala's mother and brothers had no passports. As much as Ziauddin wanted to accompany his daughter, he refused to leave the rest of the family behind, fearing they would be attacked by the Taliban. He felt terrible when he realized Malala would wake up in the hospital, in a strange country, all alone.

"Thank God, I'm Not Dead"

Malala regained consciousness on October 16. The first thing she thought was, "Thank God, I'm not dead."[40] She had a tube in her neck to help her breathe and could not speak. Malala had many questions. She had no idea where she was, how she got there, or even if her name was still Malala. And she was frightened because she did not see her parents—or even know if they were alive.

Young Pakistani students pray for Malala's recovery just days after a Taliban gunman tried to silence the outspoken teenager. News of the shooting spread quickly worldwide.

Kayani later said he would never forget the look of fear and bewilderment on Malala's face. A female Muslim chaplain came to Malala and provided some relief, praying with her and reciting verses of the Quran in Urdu. Later a nurse showed her an atlas and pointed to the hospital's location in Birmingham. Malala was also given a pink notebook so that she could communicate by writing down her questions. This is when she learned that she had been shot and that her parents were alive and well.

Over the next few days, Malala experienced a great deal of pain despite the medication she was given. Her left ear bled often, and her left hand tingled. She also had difficulty controlling her thoughts. She drifted in and out of disturbing dreams, worried intensely that her parents did not know where she was, and feared they were searching for her in the streets of Mingora.

In her hazy mental condition, Malala developed a sudden obsession with money. She wondered who was paying for her hospital stay, since her father had no money. When she saw doctors conversing, she thought they were mad at her because she could not pay the hospital bill. Malala convinced herself she needed to get up and get a job so she could buy a phone to call her family. Finally, Kayani brought a phone to Malala and helped her call her father. Although she could not speak, she was happy to hear his voice. Malala was also glad to hear that, in defiance of the Taliban, Ziauddin had reopened Khushal School four days after the attack.

> *"I didn't . . . think a single bad thought about the man who shot me—I had no thoughts of revenge—I just wanted to go back to Swat."*[41]
>
> —Malala Yousafzai.

"No Thoughts of Revenge"

By the last week of October Malala was recovering, tended by some of the world's finest doctors who employed state-of-the-art equipment to heal her wounds. But she had difficulty writing and spelling, her vision was blurry, and she experienced prolonged, severe, pounding headaches. She had a small scar above her left eye, and one side of her face sagged badly where the bullet had severely damaged the nerve.

In the following days, Malala was given details of the attack. In spite of her pain, she felt a tinge of satisfaction. The Taliban had tried to kill her, but she had survived. She wished she had had the chance to speak to the man who shot her, to explain her cause to him. But Malala held no hatred in her heart: "I didn't even think a single bad thought about the man who shot me—I had no thoughts of revenge—I just wanted to go back to Swat. I wanted to go home."[41] Recovery would take at least four months, and as the days passed the dream of home seemed to drift away. One of Malala's dreams did come true, however. The attack publicized her education campaign before a global audience. Rather than stop one girl, the Taliban had actually helped shed light on the hopes of millions of girls worldwide for the education that they deserved.

Chapter Four

An International Voice of Hope

Fifteen-year-old Malala Yousafzai was moved out of the intensive care unit at Queen Elizabeth Hospital on October 25, 2012. It had been sixteen days since she was shot by a Taliban terrorist. Since that time she had traveled thousands of miles and received treatment in four hospitals. Her British doctor, Javid Kayani, was amazed by her survival: "The chances of being shot at point blank range in the head.... I don't know why she survived. The fact that she didn't die on the spot or very soon thereafter is to my mind nothing short of miraculous."[42]

Malala faced a long recovery, but she would not have to go through this period alone. Within hours of being transferred to a regular hospital room, Malala was finally reunited with her mother, father, and two brothers. It was an emotional moment. She had not cried once through days of grueling medical procedures, as her doctor Fiona Reynolds explains: "I have never seen Malala cry. She didn't even squeeze my hand when they were sticking needles into her."[43] But she wept uncontrollably at the sight of her family.

Kayani had warned Ziauddin and Toor Pekai that their daughter had a long, slow recovery ahead of her. The gunshot had caused significant damage. Even with his warnings, they were unprepared for what they saw, as Malala explains:

> They had no idea that half my face was not working and that I couldn't smile. My left eye bulged, half my hair was gone and my mouth tilted to one side as if it had been pulled down so when I tried to smile it looked more like a grimace. It was as if my brain had forgotten it had a left face. I also couldn't hear from one side, and I spoke in baby language as if I was a small child.[44]

Trending on Twitter

As Malala recovered, international attention to her plight grew. Magazines, newspapers, and websites throughout the world filed daily reports on her condition. Queen Elizabeth Hospital was flooded with requests from journalists, politicians, actors, and activists—all wishing to see and speak to Malala. A delegation of powerful government ministers arrived from the three countries that had helped her—Pakistan, Great Britain, and the United Arab Emirates. All requests for access to Malala were denied, due to her fragile condition.

> *"The chances of being shot at point blank range in the head. . . . I don't know why she survived."*[42]
>
> —Javid Kayani, Malala's doctor.

Social media users also rallied behind Malala. Within days of the shooting, a Facebook page with a petition to nominate Malala for the Nobel Peace Prize had more than ninety thousand signatures. Her name was all over Twitter, and a November 9 picture of her reading a book in her hospital room went viral. Even pop star Madonna honored Malala in her own way; when she performed at the Staples Center in Los Angeles, Madonna revealed a temporary tattoo of Malala's name inked across the small of her back.

"You Cannot Give Up"

The United Nations sought to honor Malala by designating November 10 Malala Day. But on that day Malala thought only of the surgery she would undergo the next day. On November 11 a team of doctors worked to fix the severed nerve in the left side of Malala's face so that she would be able to open and close her eye, wiggle her nose, raise her eyebrow, and smile. The operation took eight hours, and her recovery took three months. During that time, Malala spent hours every day doing facial exercises—stretching her mouth, lifting her eyebrows, and wrinkling her nose. She also worked in the gym with a physical therapist to get her arms and legs working properly.

Though her days were occupied with exercises to regain her strength, function, and mobility, Malala did not cut herself off from the outside world. In November 2012 she read a newspaper article about a seventeen-year-old girl in Pakistan who had discovered a

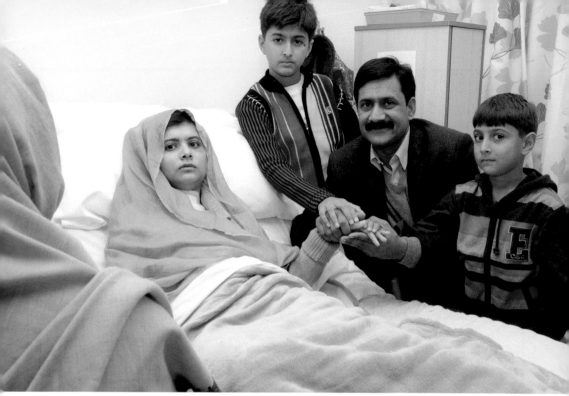

Surrounded by her family, Malala is shown recovering at Queen Elizabeth Hospital in Birmingham, England. Her doctors were amazed by her progress but warned that she faced a long, difficult recovery.

bomb under the family car. The bomb was intended for Ayesha Mir's father, Hamid Mir, a prominent Pakistani newscaster who often criticized the Taliban. According to the article, Ayesha was traumatized by the discovery and would not speak to anyone for days. On November 27 Ayesha received an unexpected phone call. "This is Malala," the caller said. "I understand that what happened was tragic, but you need to stay strong. You cannot give up."[45]

The call, made from a heavily guarded hospital room in Birmingham, England, was the only one Malala made to anyone outside her family. And it inspired Ayesha to support her father as he fought the Taliban. Malala told Ayesha to be proud, not afraid. Ayesha returned to school the next day empowered by the voice of hope from a girl who was determined to pass on her own courage and power to others.

A Titanium Skull Plate

January 3, 2013, was a momentous day for Malala. On that day she was finally discharged from the hospital. Her family had moved into

A New Home in England

When Malala Yousafzai and her family relocated to Birmingham, England, after her attack, they all experienced culture shock as they were immersed in a modern Western society for the first time. Malala describes their early experiences:

> The Pakistan High Commission had rented two serviced apartments for us in a building in a modern square in the center of Birmingham. The apartments were on the tenth floor, which was higher than any of us had ever been before....
>
> In the square was a fountain and a Costa coffee bar with glass walls through which you could see men and women chatting and mixing in a way that would be unthinkable in Swat. The apartment was just off Broad Street, a famous road of shops, night clubs and stripbars. We went to the shops though I still did not like shopping. At nights our eyes were all out on stalks at the skimpy clothes that women wore—tiny shorts almost like [underwear] and bare legs on the highest heels even in the middle of winter....
>
> We were warned not to be out late on Broad Street on weekend nights as it could be dangerous. This made us laugh. How could it be unsafe compared to where we had come from? Were there Taliban beheading people? I didn't tell my parents but I flinched if an Asian-looking man came close. I thought everyone had a gun.

Malala Yousafzai and Christina Lamb, *I Am Malala: The Story of the Girl Who Stood Up for Education and Was Shot by the Taliban*. London: Weidenfeld & Nicolson, 2013, pp. 298–99.

an apartment in central Birmingham, and doctors had determined she would be better off at home with them. The Pakistani government paid for the apartment and also picked up Malala's hospital bill, which was about $320,000. Additionally, the government hired Ziauddin as an education attaché at the Pakistani Consulate in Birmingham. In this role, Ziauddin conducted research and provided advice to Pakistani diplomats on issues concerning education.

Although she was back with her family, Malala had one more major operation to endure. On February 2 she underwent complex cranial reconstruction surgery. During the five-hour operation, called a titanium cranioplasty, doctors fitted a molded titanium plate over the hole Pakistani doctors had cut in Malala's skull after the shooting. (The original piece of bone cut from the skull and implanted in Malala's abdomen for later use was determined to be an infection risk and was not used.) The titanium plate was held in place with eight screws.

Because the hearing in Malala's left ear was lost forever, doctors also provided her with a small electronic device called a cochlear implant. The device provides a sense of sound to those who are deaf. In her typical poetic style, Malala saw the loss of hearing as a positive lesson:

We human beings don't realize how great God is. He has given us an extraordinary brain and a sensitive loving heart. He has blessed us with two lips to talk and express our feelings, two eyes which see a world of colors and beauty, two feet which walk on the road of life, two hands to work for us, a nose which smells the beauty of fragrance, and two ears to hear the words of love. As I found with my ear, no one knows how much power they have in their each and every organ until they lose one.[46]

The Man Who Shot Malala

Malala recovered quickly from the operation and was home again in five days. By this time Pakistani authorities had announced that the prime suspect in Malala's case was Ataullah Khan, a twenty-three-year-old member of the Taliban. The Pakistani government offered a 10-million-rupee reward ($105,000) for Ataullah's capture. However, it was believed that the suspect had crossed into Afghanistan after the attack; he could not be located.

In an effort to persuade Ataullah to turn himself in, Pakistani authorities arrested his mother, sister, uncle, brother, and fiancée—all of whom had nothing to do with the plot to kill Malala. Ataullah, a former college science student, was now an international outlaw. His sister, Rehana Haleem, issued a statement condemning her brother's actions:

> Please convey a message to Malala, that I apologize for what my brother did to her. He has brought shame on our family. We have lost everything after what he did.... I'd like to express my concern for Malala on behalf of my whole family; I hope she recovers soon and returns to a happy and normal life as soon as possible. I hope Malala doesn't consider me or my family as enemies. I don't consider [Ataullah] my brother anymore.[47]

In September 2014, more than two years after Malala was shot, Pakistani authorities arrested Ataullah Khan. He was convicted in an antiterrorism court and sentenced to life in prison. Mullah Fazlullah, who ordered the attack, was rumored to have been killed in a US drone strike in March 2015, but his death remains unconfirmed.

"The Extremists Are Afraid"

After the attack on Malala, the Taliban continued its terroristic campaign against the education of girls. In January 2013 the Taliban killed five teachers near the town of Swabi, about 95 miles (153 km) from Mingora. In March a forty-one-year-old teacher named Shahnaz Nazli was killed by the Taliban on her way to work at a girls' school near the town of Jamrud, about 105 miles (169 km) from Malala's hometown.

That same month, Malala returned to her own studies in a much safer environment. She joined the ninth grade class at Edgbaston High School for Girls in Birmingham. Her brothers Khushal and Atal also began attending school in the city. But as teachers and students continued to suffer in Pakistan, Malala

> *"Please convey a message to Malala, that I apologize for what my brother did to her."[47]*
>
> —Rehana Haleem, sister of Ataullah Khan, the man who shot Malala.

Sixteen-year-old Malala Yousafzai speaks at the United Nations in New York on July 12, 2013. She once again appealed for education and equality for Pakistan's girls and young women and criticized the ignorance and fear of the extremist Taliban.

felt that she needed to speak out. Her opportunity came on July 12, 2013, her sixteenth birthday.

The United Nations had designated July 12 another Malala Day, in conjunction with the first-ever Youth Takeover of the United Nations. The event brought together hundreds of young education activists from around the world. In her first public speech since the attack, Malala thanked all those who prayed for her recovery and who had sent her thousands of cards and gifts. She noted that Malala Day was not her day but the day of every woman, boy, and girl who demanded education, peace, and equality. Malala continued:

> The extremists are afraid of books and pens. The power of education frightens them. They are afraid of women. The power of the voice of women frightens them. . . . That is why they are blasting schools every day. Because they were and they are afraid of change, afraid of the equality that we will bring into our society. . . . A Talib doesn't know what is written inside [a] book. They think that God is a tiny, little conservative being who would send girls to the hell just because of going to school. The terrorists are misusing the name of Islam and Pashtun society for their own personal benefits.[48]

I Am Malala

Malala's growing fame attracted the notice of some of the most powerful leaders in the world. On October 11, 2013, Malala was invited to the White House to meet Barack Obama, First Lady Michelle Obama, and the Obamas' fifteen-year-old daughter, Malia. The United States has spent hundreds of millions of dollars building schools and supporting education programs in Afghanistan and Pakistan. Malala thanked the president for his support of education in the two countries. She also voiced her distress over ongoing US military drone strikes in Pakistan: "[I] expressed my concerns that drone attacks are fueling terrorism. Innocent victims are killed in these acts, and they lead to resentment among the Pakistani people. If we refocus efforts on education it will make a big impact."[49]

"The extremists are afraid of books and pens. The power of education frightens them. They are afraid of women. The power of the voice of women frightens them."[48]

—Malala Yousafzai.

While in the United States to meet the First Family, Malala appeared on the comedy news program *The Daily Show with Jon Stewart*. During nearly seventeen years on the show, the unflappable host had

Malala Appears on *The Daily Show*

When Malala Yousafzai appeared on the popular late-night comedy news program *The Daily Show with Jon Stewart,* she advocated for women's rights and access to education. Her answer to one of Stewart's questions left the normally garrulous host at a loss for words. Stewart asked Malala how she reacted when she learned that the Taliban wanted her dead. She said:

> I started thinking about that, and I used to think that the Talib would come, and he would just kill me. But then I said, "If he comes, what would you do Malala?" then I would reply to myself, "Malala, just take a shoe and hit him." But then I said, "If you hit a Talib with your shoe, then there would be no difference between you and the Talib. You must not treat others with cruelty and that much [harshness], you must fight others but through peace and through dialogue and through education." Then I said I will tell him how important education is and that "I even want education for your children as well." And I will tell him, "That's what I want to tell you, now do what you want."

Quoted in Brian Jones, "16-Year-Old Malala Yousafzai Leaves Jon Stewart Speechless with Comment About Pacifism," Business Insider, October 9, 2013. www.businessinsider.com.

interviewed hundreds of news makers, including presidents, politicians, rock stars, and celebrities. However, Stewart was rendered nearly speechless when Malala eloquently stated her forgiveness of the Taliban members who had tried to end her life. Stewart ended the episode by saying he was honored and humbled by Malala's presence.

Nine days after meeting the Obamas, Malala was invited to a reception at Buckingham Palace in London, where she met Queen Elizabeth and her husband, Prince Philip. Malala presented the queen with a copy of her newly published memoir, *I Am Malala: The Story of the Girl Who Stood Up for Education and Was Shot by the Taliban.* In typical Malala style, she pressed her agenda, saying she hoped the queen would use her power to make sure all children received an education.

"The Story of 61 Million Children"

By the time Malala handed her memoir to the queen, the book (co-written with British journalist Christina Lamb) was receiving international praise. Critics called the memoir fearless and riveting; reviewer Marie Arana wrote in the *Washington Post:* "It is difficult to imagine a chronicle of a war more moving."[50]

Not everyone loved *I Am Malala*, however. The All Pakistan Private Schools Federation, which claims 152,000 member institutions, banned the book, saying it disrespected Islam. Another powerful Pakistani journalist wrote that the book proved Malala was an agent against Islam working for the West. Malala was also criticized for the $3 million she was paid to write the book, which became an instant best seller.

> "I want to tell my story, but it will also be the story of 61 million children who can't get an education."[51]
>
> —Malala Yousafzai.

Malala dismissed the critics and explained why she wrote the memoir: "I hope this book will reach people around the world, so they realize how difficult it is for some children to get access to education. I want to tell my story, but it will also be the story of 61 million children who can't get an education. I want to be part of a campaign to give every boy and girl the right to go to school."[51] Toward that end, Malala used some of the money from the book to launch the Malala Fund, a foundation to empower adolescent girls through education in vulnerable communities throughout the world.

Nobel Laureate

Throughout 2014 Malala stayed busy with three roles she had taken on. She was a bookish schoolgirl in Birmingham who worried about her exams, an international spokesperson for girls' education rights, and a media sensation who appeared in numerous interviews. On October 10 Malala embarked on a new role, that of a Nobel laureate. At age seventeen she was the youngest person ever awarded

Malala Yousafzai proudly shows off her Nobel Peace Prize medal during the awards ceremony in Norway in December 2014. Building on the global goodwill and renown that her outspokenness has brought her, she continues to call for education for all of the world's young people.

the Nobel Peace Prize. (Malala was a corecipient along with Kailash Satyarthi, an Indian children's rights advocate.)

The Nobel committee noted that children and teenagers make up a large number of the populations in many of the world's poorest countries. The committee stated: "To achieve a peaceful world, it is crucial that the rights of children and young people be respected. Injustices perpetrated against children contribute to the spread of conflicts to future generations."[52] The committee explained that Malala had begun fighting for girls' rights at age eleven and continued to do so after an attack on her life by Taliban gunmen.

Malala traveled to Oslo in December to the Nobel awards ceremony, where she eloquently spoke before the king and queen of Norway and the Nobel committee. She said she was honored to be the first Pashtun and the first Pakistani to receive the award. She also said she was sure she was the first Nobel Peace Prize recipient who still fought with her younger brothers—she wanted peace everywhere but was still working it out with her siblings. The tone of Malala's speech then turned serious:

> This award is not just for me. It is for those forgotten children who want education. It is for those frightened children who want peace. It is for those voiceless children who want change. I am here to stand up for their rights, to raise their voice. . . . It is not time to pity them. It is time to take action so it becomes the last time, the last time, so it becomes the last time that we see a child deprived of education.[53]

> "To achieve a peaceful world, it is crucial that the rights of children and young people be respected."[52]
>
> —Nobel Peace Prize committee.

Malala explained that she is a stubborn person who would not rest until every woman had equal rights, every child had an education, and there was peace in every corner of the world. And Malala mentioned a number of nations besides Pakistan where her work is critically needed, including Afghanistan, Syria, Iraq, India, and Nigeria. She said the Malala Fund would receive her share of the $1.25 million prize money.

"Atrocious and Cowardly Acts"

Even as Malala spoke to the world about the desperate need for peace and education, the Taliban continued its unrelenting assault on innocent people. Less than a week after Malala's Nobel speech, Taliban gunmen stormed a school in Peshawar and went on a killing spree. The terrorists shot hundreds of teenage students, killing 141 and wounding several hundred others. Malala commented on the atrocity: "Innocent children in their school have no place in horror such as this. I am heartbroken by this senseless and cold blooded act of terror in Peshawar that is unfolding before us. . . . I condemn these atrocious and cowardly acts and stand united with the government and armed forces of Pakistan. But we will never be defeated."[54]

Malala soon found herself speaking out against another atrocity directed at young people. An Islamic fundamentalist group in Nigeria called Boko Haram kidnapped 276 schoolgirls from the town of Chibok on April 14, 2014. The group, whose name translates as "Western education is forbidden," took the girls out of their secondary school and held them as sex slaves.

In 2015, on the first anniversary of the kidnapping, Malala released an open letter to Nigeria's abducted schoolgirls offering solidarity, love, and hope. Malala said that the world would never forget them. She also revealed for the first time that she visited the parents of the girls in Nigeria and had a meeting with Nigerian president Goodluck Jonathan. Malala urged Jonathan to work harder to locate the girls and punish their captors. Malala then made a promise to the kidnapped girls:

> You will have the opportunity to receive the education you want and deserve. The Malala Fund and other organizations offered all your classmates who escaped the kidnapping full scholarships to complete their secondary education. Most of the escapee girls accepted this scholarship and are now continuing their studies at a safe boarding school and with the support they need. We hope to someday extend that same scholarship to all 219 of you, when you return home.[55]

Malala to World Leaders: "Do Better"

On the eve of receiving her Nobel Prize, Malala had published an open letter to world leaders urging them to "do better" to ensure a brighter future for all children. Malala wrote that "2015 can be a pivotal point for the world.... It can be the year in which we all commit to seeing the last child out of school, the last child forced into slavery and the last child forced to flee their home because of the danger of climate change."[56]

She continued to press for change when she made a return visit to the United States in the summer of 2015. She traveled to Washington, DC, to lobby congressional representatives to step up funding for education worldwide: "It is time that a bold and clear commitment is made by the U.S. to increase funding and support governments around the world to provide 12 years of free primary and secondary education for everyone by 2030."[57] Malala again appeared on *The Daily Show* and toured the country, speaking to sold-out crowds in Denver, Colorado; San Jose, California; and other cities. In interviews, Malala announced that a documentary about her recent activities, called *He Named Me Malala*, was in the works and slated for release in October 2015.

"We Are All Malala"

Through her work, Malala has come to understand that education is only one part of a complex puzzle that must be solved to ensure a safe, sane, and peaceful world for the most vulnerable citizens. And there are few people alive today with the eloquent voice and obvious authority necessary to move humanity toward these goals.

Malala's situation might seem unique, but as she always reminds her audiences, she represents every girl who was ever denied education, justice, or freedom of expression. Like her classmates back home, she has been empowered by pens and books. Like her friends and neighbors and other Pakistanis, she lives in fear of fanatics and remains on the Taliban hit list. And like countless others throughout history, Malala was brutally attacked after calling for basic human rights for all. Even so, she joins millions of others around the world who also reject calls for violence and revenge. Malala has become the universal girl struggling against the odds to improve her world. In the words of Pakistani cultural critic Nadeem F. Paracha: "We are all Malala."[58]

Source Notes

Introduction: She Is Malala

1. Quoted in Samira Shackle, "The Shooting of Malala Yousafzai Has Shocked Unshockable Pakistan," *New Statesman*, October 10, 2012. www.newstatesman.com.

2. Quoted in Sarah Kneezle, "Mark Your Calendars: November 10 Is 'Malala Day,'" *Time*, November 8, 2012. http://world.time.com.

3. Quoted in Kneezle, "Mark Your Calendars."

4. Quoted in Michelle Nichols, "Pakistan's Malala, Shot by Taliban, Takes Education Plea to U.N.," Reuters, July 12, 2013. www.reuters.com.

5. Quoted in Christina Boyle, "Malala Yousafzai Receives Nobel, Pleads for Education, Not War," *Los Angeles Times*, December 10, 2014. www.latimes.com.

Chapter 1: Born in a Conflicted Land

6. Malala Yousafzai and Christina Lamb, *I Am Malala: The Story of the Girl Who Stood Up for Education and Was Shot by the Taliban*. London: Weidenfeld & Nicolson, 2013, p. 14.

7. Yousafzai and Lamb, *I Am Malala*, p. 67.

8. Quoted in Yousafzai and Lamb, *I Am Malala*, p. 14.

9. Yousafzai and Lamb, *I Am Malala*, p. 15.

10. Ziauddin Yousafzai, "On World Teachers Day 2014, Malala's Inspirational Father Ziauddin Yousafzai Tells Us Why He Became a Teacher, and Why Girls' Education Is Crucial," *Malala Fund Blog*, October 4, 2014. http://community.malala.org.

11. Yousafzai, "On World Teachers Day 2014, Malala's Inspirational Father Ziauddin Yousafzai Tells Us Why He Became a Teacher, and Why Girls' Education Is Crucial."

12. Yousafzai and Lamb, *I Am Malala*, p. 56.

13. Yousafzai and Lamb, *I Am Malala*, pp. 71–72.

14. Abraham Lincoln, Facsimile Documents, Illinois Historic Preservation Agency, 2015. www.illinois.gov.

15. Quoted in Yousafzai and Lamb, *I Am Malala*, p. 84.

16. Yousafzai and Lamb, *I Am Malala*, p. 86.

17. Yousafzai and Lamb, *I Am Malala*, p. 57.

Chapter 2: The Taliban Comes to Swat Valley

18. Yousafzai and Lamb, *I Am Malala*, p. 113.

19. Quoted in Michael Daily, "Who Is Fazlullah? The Pakistani Mullah Who Targeted Malala," *Daily Beast*, November 9, 2013. www.thedailybeast.com.

20. Quoted in Daily, "Who Is Fazlullah? The Pakistani Mullah Who Targeted Malala."

21. Quoted in Daily, "Who Is Fazlullah? The Pakistani Mullah Who Targeted Malala."

22. Yousafzai and Lamb, *I Am Malala*, p. 113.

23. Yousafzai and Lamb, *I Am Malala*, p. 124.

24. Quoted in Yousafzai and Lamb, *I Am Malala*, p. 121.

25. Yousafzai and Lamb, *I Am Malala*, pp. 141–42.

26. Quoted in Tina Brown and Angelina Jolie, "Malala Speaks," *Daily Beast*, February 4, 2013. www.thedailybeast.com.

27. Malala Yousafzai, "Diary of a Pakistani Schoolgirl," BBC News, January 19, 2009. http://news.bbc.co.uk.

28. Quoted in Roslyn Peter, "Power of the Pen! 'I Am Malala,'" Donorworx, November 26 2013. www.donorworx.com.

29. Yousafzai and Lamb, *I Am Malala*, p. 161.

30. Quoted in Gary Leupp, "The Destabilization of Pakistan," *CounterPunch*, May 29–31, 2009. www.counterpunch.org.

Chapter 3: Shot for Going to School

31. Yousafzai and Lamb, *I Am Malala*, pp. 214–15.

32. Quoted in Yousafzai and Lamb, *I Am Malala*, p. 216.

33. Yousafzai and Lamb, *I Am Malala*, p. 224.

34. Yousafzai and Lamb, *I Am Malala*, p. 243.

35. Quoted in Declan Walsh, "Two Champions of Children Are Given Nobel Peace Prize," *New York Times*, October 10, 2014. www.nytimes.com.

36. Yousafzai and Lamb, *I Am Malala*, p. 244.

37. Yousafzai and Lamb, *I Am Malala*, p. 246.

38. Quoted in Basharat Peer, "The Girl Who Wanted to Go to School," *New Yorker*, October 10, 2012. www.newyorker.com.

39. Quoted in Becky Evans, "The Taliban Never Would Have Come for a Small Girl," *Daily Mail* (London), October 6, 2013. www.dailymail.co.uk.

40. Yousafzai and Lamb, *I Am Malala*, p. 275.

41. Yousafzai and Lamb, *I Am Malala*, p. 283.

Chapter 4: An International Voice of Hope

42. Quoted in Alexa Valiente, "Malala Yousafzai Continues Her Fight for Education One Year Later," ABC News, October 11, 2013. http://abcnews.go.com.

43. Quoted in Valiente, "Malala Yousafzai Continues Her Fight for Education One Year Later."

44. Yousafzai and Lamb, *I Am Malala*, p. 290.

45. Quoted in Aryn Baker, "Runner-Up: Malala Yousafzai, the Fighter," *Time*, December 19, 2012. http://poy.time.com.

46. Yousafzai and Lamb, *I Am Malala*, p. 301.

47. Quoted in Faisal Farooq, "Sister of Alleged Attacker Apologizes to Malala Yousafzai for Attack on Her," News Pakistan, November 6, 2012. www.newspakistan.pk.

48. Quoted in A World at School, "Malala Yousafzai's Speech at the Youth Takeover of the United Nations," June, 6, 2014. https://secure.aworldatschool.org.

49. Quoted in Josie Ensor, "Malala Yousafzai Meets the Obamas at the White House," *Telegraph* (London), October 12, 2013. www.telegraph.co.uk.

50. Marie Arana, "Book Review: 'I Am Malala' by Malala Yousafzai," *Washington Post*, October 11, 2013. www.washingtonpost.com.

51. Quoted in Aaron Couch, "Malala Yousafzai, Child Activist Shot by Taliban, Closes Book Deal," *Hollywood Reporter*, March 27, 2013. www.hollywoodreporter.com.

52. Nobelprize.org, "Malala Yousafzai—Facts," 2015. www.nobelprize.org.

53. Malala Yousafzai, "Nobel Lecture," Nobelprize.org, December 10, 2014. www.nobelprize.org.

54. Quoted in Brian Murphy, "Nobel Laureate Malala Yousafzai 'Heartbroken' by Pakistani School Massacre," *WorldViews* (blog), *Washington Post*, December 16, 2014. www.washingtonpost.com.

55. Quoted in Josh Levs, "Malala's Letter to Nigeria's Abducted Schoolgirls: 'Solidarity, Love, and Hope," CNN, April 13, 2015. www.cnn.com.

56. Malala Yousafzai, "Malala Yousafzai Challenges World Leaders to 'Do Better,'" *Mail & Guardian* (Johannesburg, South Africa), December 10, 2014. http://mg.co.za.

57. Quoted in Danielle Haynes, "Malala Yousafzai Lobbies on Capitol Hill for Global Education Funding," UPI, June 23, 2015. www.upi.com.

58. Nadeem F. Paracha, "Why Can't Pakistanis Condemn the Taliban for Shooting a 14-Year-Old Girl?," *Foreign Policy*, October 10, 2012. http://foreignpolicy.com.

Important Events in the Life of Malala Yousafzai

1997

Malala Yousafzai is born on July 12 in Mingora, Pakistan.

1999

Malala's brother Khushal is born.

2001

The United States invades Afghanistan on October 7; thousands of Taliban fighters escape to Pakistan.

2002

Malala starts attending school.

2003

The Taliban sets up training camps in Pakistan, which leads to the group gaining control of the country's Pashtun tribal region.

2004

After encountering a young girl scavenging for food in a garbage pile, Malala pledges to one day help all street children go to school.

2007

The Taliban takes control of the Swat Valley, where Malala and her family live.

2008

Malala is interviewed for the first time by ATV Khyber, the only Pashtun television station. She soon appears on GEO, the most-watched news channel in Pakistan.

2009

Under the pseudonym Gul Makai, Malala writes a blog for the BBC called *The Diary of a Pakistani Schoolgirl*, which describes her feelings after the Taliban orders all girls' schools closed.

2010

Malala appears on a popular Pakistani television news show.

2011

Malala becomes a national hero after winning Pakistan's National Youth Peace Prize and telling an interviewer she is afraid of no one.

2012

On October 9, while riding the bus home from school, Malala is shot in the head by Taliban member Ataullah Khan.

2013

Malala's memoir, *I Am Malala: The Story of the Girl Who Stood Up for Education and Was Shot by the Taliban*, is published.

2014

Malala becomes the youngest person ever to receive the Nobel Peace Prize. The award money goes into the Malala Fund, a foundation to empower adolescent girls through education.

2015

Malala meets with politicians in Washington, DC, seeking a US commitment to provide twelve years of free education for all children everywhere by 2030.

For Further Research

Books

Stuart A. Kallen, *The War in Afghanistan*. San Diego: ReferencePoint, 2013.

Natalie Maydell and Sep Riahi, *Extraordinary Women from the Muslim World*. Seattle: Global Content, 2014.

David Nelson, ed., *Afghanistan*. Farmington Hills, MI: Greenhaven, 2013.

Lauri S. Scherer, ed., *The Taliban*. Farmington Hills, MI: Greenhaven, 2013.

Sean Sheehan, *Pakistan*. New York: Cavendish Square, 2015.

Malala Yousafzai and Christina Lamb, *I Am Malala: The Story of the Girl Who Stood Up for Education and Was Shot by the Taliban*. London: Weidenfeld & Nicolson, 2013.

Internet Sources

BBC News, "Who Are the Taliban?," November 1, 2013. www.bbc .com/news/world-south-asia-11451718.

Human Rights Watch: "World Report 2015: Pakistan," 2015. www .hrw.org/world-report/2015/country-chapters/pakistan.

New York Times, "Malala Yousafzai's Surgery," video, 2015. www.ny times.com/video/world/asia/100000002033980/malala-yousafzais -surgery.html.

Websites

Global Campaign for Education (www.campaignforeducation.org). The Global Campaign for Education believes education is a basic human right and works to end what it calls the global education crisis. The site contains student blogs, current events in education, and information about campaigns to train teachers, expand girls' education, and promote literacy for all.

Malala Fund (www.malala.org). The website for the endowment set up by Malala Yousafzai to empower girls throughout the world through quality secondary education. The site follows Malala's latest public activities for the cause and publishes her blogs as well as those by other education activists.

Malala Yousafzai Blog & Story (www.malala-yousafzai.com). This site features Malala Yousafzai's biography, the full diary she wrote for the BBC, and the speech she gave after receiving the Nobel Prize. The site also contains articles about Malala, student letters she has received, and even a music video about her.

Right to Education Project (www.right-to-education.org). The project was established in 2008 as a collaboration between several international aid groups, including Amnesty International and Save the Children. The site features blogs, news, and extensive information about education in emergencies, free education, and marginalized groups in developing nations.

Rotary Mingora Swat (www.rotarymingora.org). This site provides detailed information about the history, languages, demographics, and culture of Malala's hometown and the Swat District where it is located.

United Nations Girls' Education Initiative (UNGEI!) (www.ungei.org). Launched in 2008, UNGEI! has a vision of a world where all girls and boys receive quality education. The site features numerous blogs from students the organization has helped throughout the world.

Index

Edgbaston High School for Girls, 56
education
  of girls   attacked by Boko Haram in Nigeria, 63
    effect of Malala's shooting on, 50
    father's belief in importance of, 14
    and Malala as student, 16
    Taliban attacks on, **29**, 29–30, 32, 56
    Taliban ban, 6, 32, 34
  in madrassas, 23, 26
  of Malala and her brothers in England, 56
  Malala's activism for, 37–38
    Malala Fund and, 9, 60, 62
    media interviews about, 31–32, 58–59
    meeting with Queen Elizabeth and Prince Philip and, 59–60
    and memoir, 60
    in Nigeria, 63
    in United States, 58–59, 63–64
  Malala's desire for, 6
  of poor people, 18–19, 39
  power of, 58
Ehsan, Ehsanullah, 45
Ellick, Adam, 34
England
  education in, 56
  home in Birmingham, 54
  meeting with Queen Elizabeth andPrince Philip of, 59–60
  treatment in, 48–53, **53**
environmental conditions in Pakistan, 19–20

Falcon Commandos, 27
Fazlullah
  appeal of, to women, 24–25
  and attack on Malala, 45

and closing of schools for girls, 32, 34
education of, 26
radio broadcasts by, 24, 25, 29–30
unconfirmed death of, 56
on women as subservient to men, 30
First Battle of Swat, 28–30, **29**
flogging, 27

Gilani, Yousaf Raza, 38, **39**
girls
  education of
    attacked by Boko Haram in Nigeria, 63
    effect of Malala's shooting on, 50
    father's belief in importance of, 14
    and Malala as student, 16
    Taliban attacks on, **29**, 29–30, 32, 56
    Taliban ban, 6, 32, 34
  low status of, 11
  purdah and, 31
  Taliban restrictions on, 6, 21
Global Peace Council, 42
Gul Makai (pseudonym), 33

Haleem, Rehana, 56
He Named Me Malala (documentary), 63–64
hero, defined, 6
honor *(nang)*, importance of, in *Pashtunwali*, 11

I Am Malala (Yousafzai), 59, 60
imams, 13
Institute for War & Peace Reporting, 37
Islam
  fundamentalist, 23, 26, 63
  leaders, 13, 23–24

Picture Credits

About the Author

Stuart A. Kallen is the author of more than three hundred nonfiction books for children and young adults. He has written on topics ranging from the theory of relativity to the art of animation. In addition, Kallen has written award-winning children's videos and television scripts. In his spare time he is a singer, songwriter, and guitarist in San Diego.